Mayo Park

The Inception

Robert W. Haeussinger

Mayo Park has been part of Rochester since 1906, some one hundred and twelve years. Its formative years were plagued with setbacks, none bigger than the flood of June 1908. On a proportional scale, it's was large as the flood of 1978. Following the flood of 08, civic leaders took the necessary steps to prevent future damage, the flood of 1911, a testimony to those efforts. The city did the same following the 1978 flood.

The story here is about those early days, from conception through 1911. Specifically, how the city transformed a flood prone area into a civic amenity of beauty, and it survives to this day. At the start of the 20th Century, Rochester was a 'cosmopolitan' frontier, slowly but surely moving away from its rural heritage, while retaining certain attributes of a frontier environment. The Park was a place where people could go to and relax, free from the burdens of the day-the peaceful setting of Mayo Park.

The idea for community parks dates back many years. In the 1850's Fredrick Law Olmsted, the well renowned landscape architect and land use planner designed what would eventually become Central Park in New York City. The park opened to the public in 1857. For the remainder of the century "The City Beautiful Movement" swept across the country. Following the World Exposition at the 1893 Chicago World's Fair, beautification efforts really took off and gave rise to efforts in Rochester. The basic premise of the movement, cities must have space set aside where residents can relax and have fun, free from stench, poverty, and the business of the city. Rochester and Olmsted County grew rapidly once the railroad arrived in 1864, however streets were little more than dirt paths. At night, the city was cloaked in darkness except for a scattering of kerosene lamps. During winter, the air filled with black smoke, coal and wood being the primary source of heat. Rochester, like many Midwestern communities in the late 1800's, was rustic and unsettled, change, ever constant.

In 1871 a company whose name is unknown, proposes to build a dam a across the Zumbro River at 4th Street SE (then called College Street); current the parking lot were the Farmers Market is held each summer. The company planned to generate power from the resultant water surge. However, the City Council rejects the idea. The following year, 1872, Mayor William W. Mayo (a.k.a. Dr. Mayo) wages a 'terrific fight' to have a dam built on the same site and thus form a lake and a park site farther downstream. The idea was abandoned when a landscape architect reported quicksand present at the site would make the project prohibitively expensive. (A waterworks plant is later built at that same site, following construction of the dam on the north end of Silver Lake).

For the next thirty plus years, the idea of developing a park for the city remained dormant. The economic boom of the 1870's, turn into an economic disaster in the 1880's. Additional markets for the expanding agricultural economy had failed to materialize, prices paid for farm products plummet as a result. Farmers unable to pay the mortgage, abandon the land and moved on. Land values fell as a result. The population gains realized in the 1860's and 1870's, all but wiped out. The financial crash of 1893 also has a dramatic impact on the area. Despite all of that, things start to improve, be it ever slowly. Early in the 20th century, people in the community take up the idea of a park. Dr. William and Dr. Charles Mayo and John R. Cook all play a significant role in that effort.

In early 1904, the three men (together) put up $6,000 of their own money to purchase the necessary land for the new park (Mayo's share, $5,000; Cook's, $1,000). Originally, the thought was to buy eleven acres although sixteen acres were added a short time later, encompassing some sixteen square blocks. Initially the City Council rejects the idea of acquiring the needed land, thinking the estimated cost of $12,000 was simply 'too' much. Their position changed, following a community wide meeting the night of June 30, 1904.

A large gathering of key civic and business leaders and local citizens meet at the Metropolitan Theatre (presently the site of the Post Office on Broadway); the topic, Mayo

Park. Mr. C. M. Loring, a landscape architect and park designer from Minneapolis was the principal speaker. The Commercial Club and the Merchants Association invited him to speak at the gathering, principally; Mr. J.F. Reid personally contacted Mr. Loring. Loring talked at length about how a park would be a real asset for the community. Given the suggested location, further amenities were possible. At the conclusion of the presentation, the consensus was to 'build it'. That gave Council the political support they need to act.

The City Council subsequently votes to amend the City Charter therein creating the Municipal Park Board. The Board's job was to oversee the construction and manage the grounds when completed. In making its decision, the Council orders the land be condemned for public purpose and calculate the relative value of each parcel acquired.

The owners subject to condemnation and the 'assessed' value: Wm. Fraser $300; Lizzie Dale $350; W.F. Friedell $150; Mary J. Franklin $75; D avid B. Franklin $425; A.T. Stebbins $850; J.A. Leonard $150; Rose M. Hall $748; Anna Volz $300; S.O. Sanderson $290; the heirs of George Bailey $234; the First National Bank, Bailey's mortgage holder $1,020; and $696.50 for an aggregate of small substandard parcels. In cases where the property owner wished to remove a structure from his or her parcel, the money given them would be reduced accordingly.

In late July 1906, Frank Nutter, a well-known landscape engineer from Minneapolis, arrives in the city. The Park Board hired him to coordinate work activities relative to the proposed layout. Figure 1 is the initial (i.e. proposed) layout for Mayo Park (for clarification, identifying text and color was added). The perimeter of the Park consists of Fifth, Cherry, and College Streets. The dotted blue line on the left side of the diagram indicates the course of the river in 1882. The plan, have that path become the main course thru, thus allowing Zumbro Street to continue east and act as an entrance to the park. Dubuque Street will be extended and a bridge 'placed' over the river. A small bridge across the lagoon at the end of Fourth Street is also considered. You'll also notice a driveway will extend from College Street west on Cherry Street, connect at Zumbro Street and then head on to Fifth Street (a.k.a. Center Street). The part from Zumbro to Fifth is now called Mayo Park Drive. The access points will allow for multiple entrances. The 'Island' will remain unchanged, given its natural beauty and given it's subject to annual flooding following rapid snow melting. Figure 2 identifies the streets as they appear today. The public's reaction to the proposed design was overwhelming; they looked forward to it with great anticipation. The matter of completing the park rests with the Park Board.

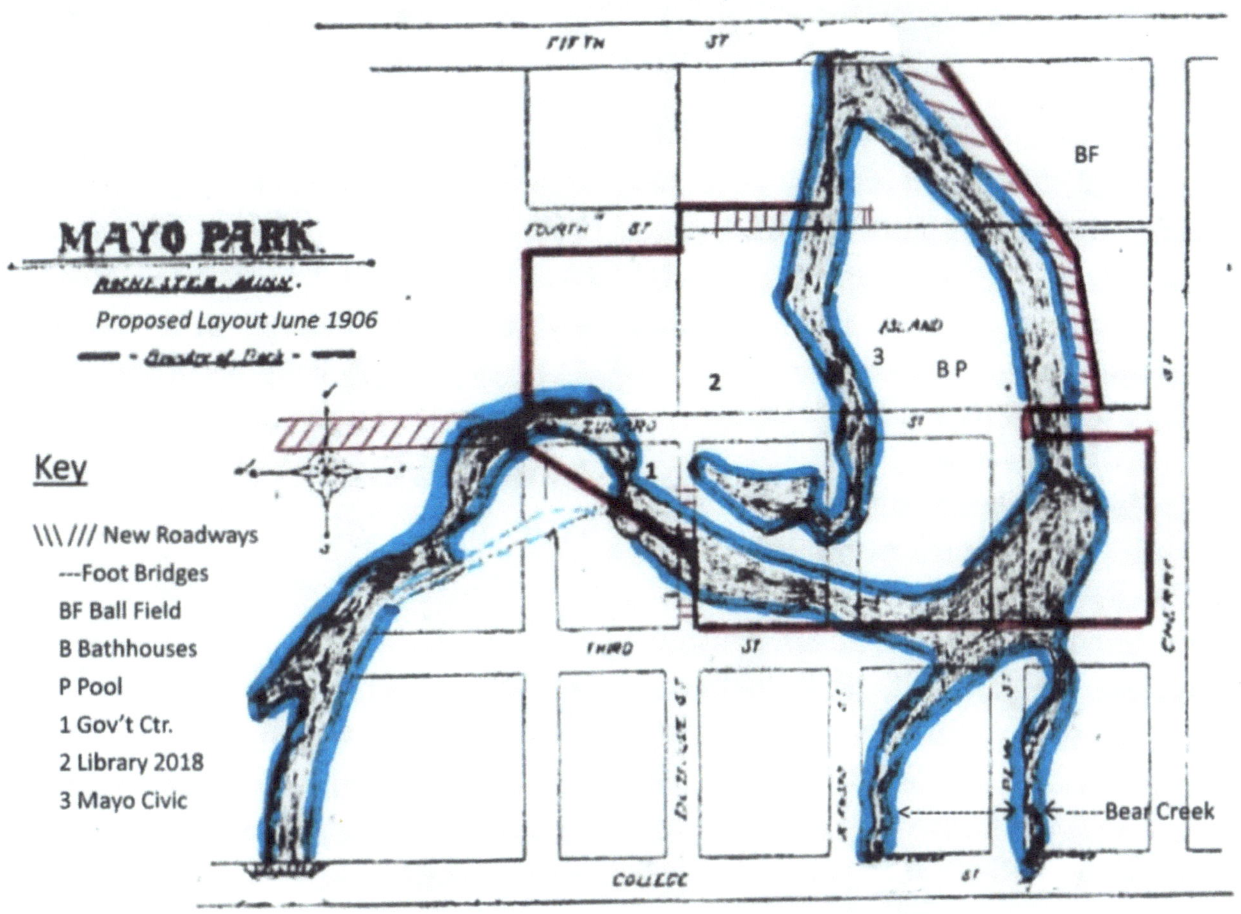

Figure 1: 1906 Proposal

Key: Red Line, Proposed Border; Blue Line, River Channel(s);

Dotted Light Blue Line 1882 Channel and the Channel in Use Today

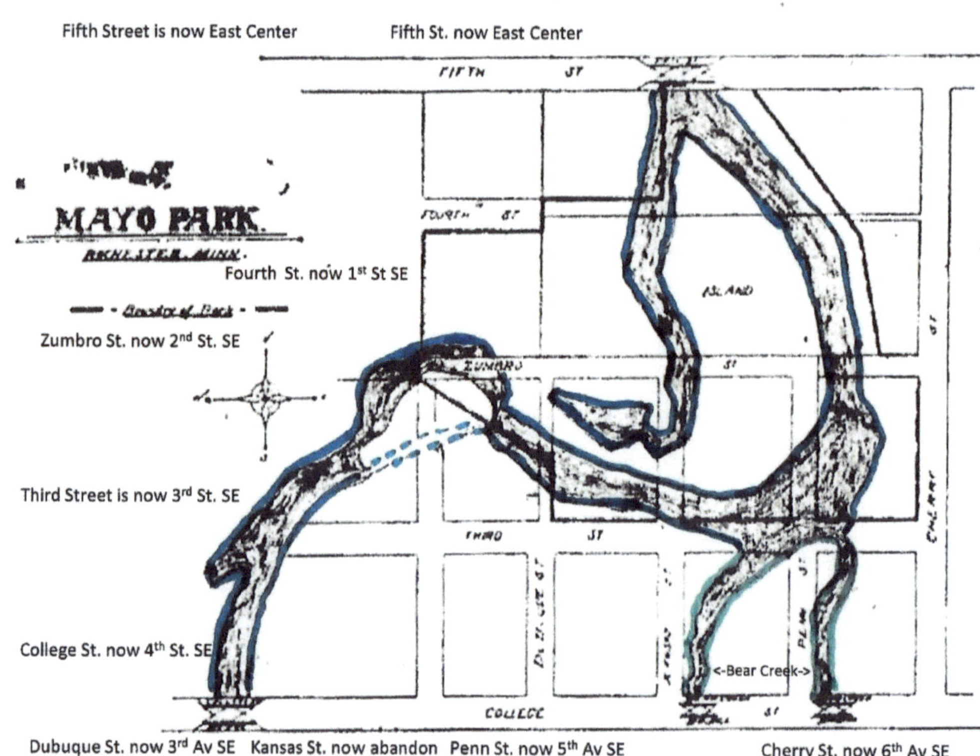

Figure 2
Old Street / New Street Names

The Board is comprised of four members, Phil G. Heintz, John M. Rowley, Albert S. Whiting and Thomas Spillane (Spillane replaced the late Logan Brackenridge). The bathhouse project was the first major item up for discussion, following acquisition.

In July 1907, the Park Board receives plans for the bathhouse, it will be located on the 'Island'. The building, as proposed, would be seventy-eight feet in length and will include all the features of an 'up-to-date' bathhouse. The dressing rooms will accommodate up to one hundred bathers. The building will be located near the shoreline where the water depth would be conducive for water sports. The structure will face Fifth (a.k.a. Center) Street. Construction bids will arrive within soon.

A week later, the Park Board reconvenes; the Board wasn't satisfied with the bids submitted. As such, they elect to take a different path. First, they direct a Martin Heffron to visit the Twin Cities and study the public baths now in operation. Upon his return, new plans were drawn up. This time, construction would be handled differently. Instead of letting bids for the project, the Board will coordinate construction, i.e. buy the necessary materials and then hire the appropriate and necessary labor. The Board felt this would save a 'considerable' amount of money. The community backs their decision 100%. The bathhouse will be located on the north end of the island and 'viewed' from Fifth (a.k.a. Center) Street. The building will be a framed structure measuring 48 x 28 feet and face north. Fifth Street will serve as a 'grandstand' from which to 'watch' the bathers. The building itself will consist of two sections, one for men and boys, the other for women and girls; each section will have its own entrance.   Each section will have changing areas. On the men / boys' side, there'll be thirty-three dressing rooms; on the women/girls' side twenty-five. At the front of the building, steps will lead down to the water. The structure will also be elevated five feet above the surrounding ground; construction will take no more than a month. As work on the building moves ahead, several residents talk about forming a tennis club. Their idea, layout dirt courts within the Park. At least a dozen men and half as many women agree to purchase necessary equipment. Nature had different ideas the following Spring, June 1908.

1882 was the last time flood waters struck the city. Now fast-forward twenty-six years. Inside two hours, the creek and river channel rose from an insignificant stream to a raging torrent. Much like the 1978 flood, it was a wet spring, especially in the days leading up to the event. Between seven and eight the morning of the 26th, the water rose some four feet in less than twenty minutes. In the case of the '78' flood, the heavy rain started around seven o'clock the night before. In 1908, the rain started at 11:30 the night before (i.e. the 25th). In 1908, the flood peaked around 9:30 AM and an hour later the water starts to recede, be ever so slowly. The damage was horrific; Mayo Park was totally decimated. The course of the flood followed the 1882 channel (i.e. the area bordered by the dotted light blue lines identified in Figure 1).

The Park bathhouse, not yet a year old, destroyed; just a single door remained on the island, the rest of the building, scattered downstream. They even found a large section on the wall west of Oakwood Cemetery. Three smaller bathhouses would be built to take the place of the original. Of the six boats moored in the Park, only three were found but only one was intact, one was broken in half and third one had its bow missing. Only one piece of the recently installed swing set was left behind. Even the merry-go-round, a real treasure for the young people, got destroyed. Virtually none of Park escaped nature's wrath. At one time or another during the flood, nearly every part of the Park was covered with water. The challenge, finding the money to rebuild. Community leaders said, "…the effort needed to rebuild should not be curtailed by financial constraints.   The initial task, restore the banks and shorelines decimated by the flood. The goal, build them to withstand future events, i.e. floods. The following pictures are from the 1908 flood.

City Waterworks Building @ 423 College St (4ᵗʰ Street SE)
A Few Weeks before the Flood

**City Water Works Plant looking from the northwest, a day later
423 College Street (4th Street SE)**

The Old Mill Looking to the Southwest

Schuster Brewery at College (4th St. SW) and Main Street (1st Av SW) Looking Across the Channel towards the SW. The River Flows from Right to Left

Recovering from the flood's effects proves a huge undertaking, but city leaders and the business community were determined to make it work. Shorelines needed to be rebuilt, as would the bathhouse and the accompanying beach, swimming and boat areas. To prevent further erosion, 408 bundles of 'mattress willows were brought in from Winona and placed at strategic points as were large amounts of rock. To lift community spirits, the old Civil War cannon resting atop College Hill (i.e. the park directly behind St. Mary's Hospital) was relocated to Mayo Park as a civic reminder of the city's heritage. Prior to its retirement from active use, the cannon was fired off every 4th of July promptly at dawn.

A year after the flood, foot races come to the Park. Boys and girls ages five to sixteen participate. Races include, the 25, 40, 50, and 100-yard runs. Additional contests include a three-legged race, a boy's sack race, a girl's potato race, a wheelbarrow race; and topping the day, a quarter mile run. Unfortunately, progress in restoring the natural beauty of the Park, constrained by dry weather and limited resources (money). Things begin to improve by the spring of 1910.

In late June, the City announces two marble statues will be coming to the Park real soon. The noted Italian sculptor Antonio Frilli will craft statutes of Presidents Washington and Lincoln. Drs. William and Charles Mayo ordered and paid for those masterpieces while visiting overseas. They will be a gift to the city. The statues should arrive sometime during the month of September; improvements continue unabated.

In August, cement sidewalk is placed along the Fifth (Center) Street frontage that parallels the park. The grade will allow it to match up with the adjoining bridge elevation. Signposts will follow shortly thereafter. They will tell drivers to stay to the 'right'. Quoting one official, "a careless chauffeur or driver of horses might 'easily' get in trouble if they do not observe the laws of the road." Also, that same month 30,000 yearling crappies were dropped into the river to restore fishing *opportunities*. Screens would be put in place to prevent fish from entering the Mill intakes. Fishing laws will be strictly enforced, no game fish under six inches in length can be taken, minnow seining is forbidden. In time,

Rochester would become an ideal place to fish. In the fall of 1910, plans got underway to develop Mayo Field.

In the 1906 proposed plan, a ball field was targeted for the area south of Fifth (Center) Street and west what is now Mayo Park Drive. Unfortunately, that area was quite small, the area immediately across Fifth Street and beside Oakwood Cemetery was a suggested alternative. The site, as proposed, would offer multiple venues for everyone. Baseball, football, racing, handball, tennis and croquet were among the permitted activities.

The concrete grandstand would seat 5,000 people, its placement, at the south side of the field facing north. Behind the grandstand will be a handball court. Around the perimeter of the field will be a quarter mile track available for area schools. Behind the baseball, diamond will lay the football field. In the center of the football field will be a basketball court. Three tennis and a single croquet court would be located beyond the outfield. Along the riverbank, several clubhouses would be erected; each containing lockers and shower facilities. North of the clubhouses, exhibition buildings would be built for use during the county fair. During other times, the buildings would be open to other groups. As of late October, `the final design awaits approval; work could begin the following spring.

The Athletic Board assumes a host of organizations within the region will take advantage of the offerings. The high school athletic association will most likely use Mayo Field for its football and baseball games. Parochial schools in the area were welcome as well. Whether the Fair Board elects to use the site for the County Fair remains uncertain, there isn't enough room to accommodate a horseracing event.

Proponents believe Mayo Field it will contribute as much to the community as will Mayo Park once fully developed. Rochester assuredly will become a leader in outdoor sporting events for youth and adults with the availability of Mayo Park and the eventually construction of Mayo Field. It's only a matter of time. In December 1910, the statues arrive at Mayo Park.

On December 14, the statue of George Washington is put in place on a three-foot pedestal situated in the plaza. At the base of the statue are inscribed the words "Presented to the City of Rochester by the Mayo Family, November 30, 1910". The statute of Washington stands upright, his weight leans on his right foot which rests on a tree stump. His saber hangs from his left side, his right arm slightly bent, his fingers rest on the lapel of his jacket. The general's shoulder epaulets accent his military prowess and dominate character. The formal unveiling and dedication will occur later. The statue of President Abraham Lincoln arrives the next day. Statues weren't the only things coming to the Park.

Mr. Andrew Seeverts of Byron graciously donates the William Dee house (a house he presently owns) to the City for eventually placement in Mayo Park. The log cabin, one of the three first built in the city; they date back to 1862. Dee planned to make it home for his young bride, but later sells it and moves away. In the coming years, the building is moved several times, while in the Park. When the building is moved the final, it's placed behind the Olmsted County History Center, where it resides today. A copy of Dr. Mayo's thank you letter to Mr. Seeverts follows.

                    DR. WILLIAM J. MAYO
                       Rochester,Minn.

                                        July 4,1911.

Mr.Andrew Seeverts,
    Byron, Minn.

My dear Mr. Seeverts:

            I want to thank you most heartily in the name of

my mother, my sister, my brother and myself, for your gift of the

oldest house in Rochester to Mayo Park.

            We all fully realize that this gift was made by you

in memory of my father, who was one of your personal friends for 6ver

forty years, and as the park is dedicated to him, we are very glad to

have the old log house come to the park from one of his old and valued

friends.

            We assure you of our appreciation.

                            Very sincerely yours,

                            W.J.Mayo.

Note: The log cabin referred to, was originally built by Wm. Dee, on High Street,
      in Spring of 1862, for his bride. Consisted of two rooms and a loft.
      This was the 3rd log cabin built in Rochester.   It is the only remaining
      original log cabin of the pioneer period.   Mrs.B.T.Willson.
      See history for further data.

William Dee Log Cabin at the History Center

In the spring of 1911, the Park Board for the City of Rochester receives a $5,000 donation from the promoters of Mayo and College Hill Park. The money, earmarked to beautify the *landscape* at each location. Subsequently, the Board acquires the services of Mr. C. E. Greening, a landscaper architect from Monroe Michigan, to coordinate and complete all the necessary work. Hopefully the work will be done by fall, weather permitting.

'THE ISLAND' LOOKING SOUTH--NOTE THE WATER WORKS TOWER

ZUMBRO (2nd STREET SE) BRIDGE

WEST CHANNEL OF THE ZUMBRO RIVER
MCC AREA RIGHT AND PAST THE BRIDGE, RIGHT OF THE TREES

EARLY FOOT BRIDGE EXACT LOCATION UNKNOWN

LOW WATER WEST CHANNEL, YEAR UNKNOWN

NOTE THE DOCKED ROW BOATS, SIX AVAILABLE FOR RENTAL

SWIMMING OFF THE 'ISLAND'

PARK PLAYGROUND/ACTIVITY AREA

Early Plaza Area

The Very First Bathhouse, Destroyed in the 1908 Flood

NEWLY BUILT BATHHOUSES FOLLOWING THE 1908 FLOOD

DEER PRESERVE

Mayo Park Drive

Old Civil War Cannon

MCC
****
Eastern Portion of Original Island

THE TAYLOR AND MAYO ARENAS AND A PORTION OF THE TREES MAKE UP MUCH OF THE 'ISLAND' FOOTPRINT

ZUMBRO RIVER CHANNEL TODAY, ONCE THE EAST CHANNEL

**ZUMBRO RIVER LOOKING UP RIVER TO THE SOUTH
THE ART CENTER ON THE RIGHT HALFWAY DOWN**

BEAR CREEK LOOKING SOUTH (UP CREEK)

NEW CONSTRUCTION OVERLOOKING THE PARK

MAYO PARK DRIVE LOOKING TOWARDS THE CENTER STREET BRIDGE
THE SAME DRIVE PROPOSED IN 1906

THE SE CORNER OF THE PARK AS PROPOSED IN 1906
TODAY THE CORNER OF 4TH STREET & 6TH AVENUE SE

Memorial Day of 1911, ceremonies commence at Oakwood Cemetery and at Mayo Park. The service at Oakwood honors the brave young men who fought and died in the Civil War and to those veterans who survived. Reading of Lincoln's Gettysburg Address concludes the service. Following that, activities shift to Mayo Park. There the statues of Washington and Lincoln are officially turned over to the city. Mayor Richardson formally accepts them on behalf of the city. Members of the Grand Army of the Republic (named for the men who fought for the North during the Civil War) are among the invited guests. Charles Van Campen, Commander of Custer Post, speaks on the soldiers' behalf. His comments are then directed to Drs. William and Charles Mayo. The ceremony proves a moving experience. The statues thus solidify Mayo Park's position within the history of Rochester. The beauty of the Park does not escape the attention of a former resident who happens to visit the Park a short time later.

The Rev. Frank Doran visits the Park early in July 1911 following a long absence. During his brief stay, he takes time to stroll through the place he once referred as the 'barnyard'. The place where city tools and electrical poles were once stored and on occasion, the site of questionable markets, e.g. ad hoc flea markets, but now it's a place of beauty. He finds the recreation area with its fountains, flowers, vines of numerous varieties and assortment of trees all quite fascinating. The statues and the old cannon remind him of the city's heritage. No place is more popular in the summer than the banks of the Zumbro. Three years earlier, a horrendous flood devastated the Park. The flood fortunately does not destroy the large oaks, which in full bloom have a beauty second to none. Later that month, a note of sadness, deer in the Park's reserve die unexpectedly. Come October floodwaters return. When the rains start, residents recall that awful day in June 1908. This time the outcome is much different. Following the 08 flood, city leaders chose to reinforce the riverbanks within the Park and at select sites down river. Except for the 'automobile' road and gravel walkway, which got washed out, and the footbridges moved out of position, no significant destruction occurs. Come midnight, the River peaks and then slowly recedes; total damage around $200. Even Dubuque Street (3rd Avenue SE) escapes unscathed; it previously sustained heavy damage in 1908.

By the mid-1920s, Rochester experiences a transformation of sort, something that changes the direction of the Park to a certain degree. For many, change is hard to accept. That change is the topic for another time. The Park, from its inception, had numerous setbacks, but survived through persistence, hard work and determination by community leaders; without question, their contribution is commendable. Today, strangers from all over the world visit the park and marvel at its beauty.

I wish to thank the volunteers and staff at the Olmsted County History Center in helping me assemble material for this book.

Newspaper Citations

Year	Month	Day	Paper	Page	Column
1904	7	1	PR	2	
1906	3	16	PR	1	6
1906	7	20	PR	7	1
1907	7	12	OCD	5	2
1907	7	19	OCD	5	5
1907	8	2	PR	8	3
1908	6	26	OCD	1	1
1908	6	26	OCD	4	6
1908	8	7	OCD	5	3
1909	6	18	OCD	5	1
1909	7	2	PR	3	1
1910	7	1	PR	7	1
1910	7	1	PR	4	4
1910	8	5	PR	1	4
1910	10	14	PR	2	3
1910	12	16	PR	1	5
1911	6	30	OCD	2	
1911	7	21	OCD	1	3
1911	6	2	PR	7	1
1911	7	7	OCD	3	1
1911	10	20	OCD	1	3
1912	6	7	PR	1	7
1912	8	2	PR	2	6

Paper ID: OCD = Olmsted County Democrat; PR = Post Record